PRAYING YOU GOODBYE

A CHRISTIAN'S COMPANION IN GRIEVING, HEALING, AND GRATITUDE

MAUREEN RYAN GRIFFIN

PHOTOGRAPHY BY WENDY H. GILL

Photographs by Wendy H. Gill.
See more of her work at
facebook.com/whgillphotography.

Author photograph by Donna Foster Photography
at www.donnafoster.com.

Published in the United States of America by

FLOATING LEAF PRESS

A division of
WordPlay
Maureen Ryan Griffin
6420 A-1 Rea Road, Suite 218, Charlotte, NC 28277
Phone: 704-494-9961
Email: info@wordplaynow.com
www.wordplaynow.com

Library of Congress Control Number: 2017907070
Rev. Ed. of: Praying You Goodbye.
Expanded, with photographs.

ISBN 978-0-9802304-3-7

For my mother,
Patricia Colette Brachowski Ryan

I will never forget you.

ACKNOWLEDGMENTS

All Scripture quotations are from the New International Version, unless otherwise noted.

Thanks to the editors/publishers of the following in which these writings first appeared:

The Chautauquan Daily: "The Last of Your Pond's Skin Cream"
Crucible: "When the Leaves Are in the Water"
Mount Olive Review: "The Color of Crushed Strawberries"
They Wrote Us a Poem VIII: "When We Parted, All That Was Really Left"
Wellspring: "For Mother, as I Sort Through This Old Box of Clothes Saved for a Granddaughter"

Spinning Words into Gold: "All week, I have been wanting to write about..." (Main Street Rag Publishing Company, 2006)
Ten Thousand Cicadas Can't Be Wrong: "Leaves, Wind, Light, Wings" (Main Street Rag Publishing Company, 2014)

Much gratitude to the Sisters of Mercy and Well of Mercy staff, particularly Sister Brigid McCarthy and Sister Donna Marie Vaillancourt, for their vision, their love, and their hospitality. Their ministry is a blessing to many, and provided the comfort and solitude needed to create this book. Find out more about Well of Mercy at www.wellofmercy.org.

Special thanks to Wendy H. Gill, who provided valuable insight and support throughout this book's creation, as well as the beautiful photographs that grace its pages; Reverend Rebecca Taylor for her faith, vision, encouragement, and help with content and Scriptural quotations; Judy Huitt for her Scriptural contributions; and Doug McVadon for his generosity in sharing the distinctions of Landmark Education, which continue to make such a difference in my life. As always, I am grateful to my family and friends for their ongoing love and support.

CONTENTS

HOW THIS BOOK CAME TO BE

I first created this farewell ritual at a retreat center in Hampton-ville, North Carolina, called Well of Mercy, in June, 2002, shortly after my mother died.

I was blessed to have my mother for forty-five years, long enough to move through the pain left over from my childhood (my mother struggled with depression and anxiety, diseases which take a toll on many families) and to come to appreciate what a wonderful mother she was. She gave so much to me and my siblings—physically and spiritually. I was doubly blessed to have been able to spend time with her during what we both knew was the end of her life. By that time, I'm grateful to say, what was left between us was love—simple, clean, pure. And yet, loss is never easy, regardless of the circumstances. I still had regrets, fear, and even anger, and the deep grief of knowing that my life would never be the same without her physical presence in it.

All the conversations I'd had with others about her weren't enough to assuage this loss. All the writing I'd done to express my mix of emotions wasn't enough. Even having spent her last night on earth with her, listening to her breath enter and leave her body—even knowing that my last words to her were "Perry Como is waiting in heaven to sing to you"—wasn't enough.

I had more to tell her, more to understand, experience, and release. This ritual provided the peace, acceptance, and closure I needed, and it opened a new, deeper relationship with the mother that I would forever carry inside me.

While I shed many tears as I walked Well of Mercy's Prayer Path saying goodbye to her, in the end my primary emotion was gratitude—for Well of Mercy itself and its healing peace, for the gift of quiet time to honor my love for my mother, and for the gift of my mother's presence in my life. How good it was to have a place in which I could retreat from the cares and concerns of my everyday life to let myself feel my grief, to choose what I would hold onto and what I would let go of.

My ritual would have ended right there, if not for my friend Rebecca Taylor, to whom I'd mentioned this process. She lost her father not long after I'd lost my mother, and asked if I'd be willing to share my ritual with her. I was happy to, and painstakingly wrote out what I'd done, along with a few examples. That was that, I thought, glad I could help her. But Rebecca, a Presbyterian minister, had other plans. She'd shown the simple pamphlet I'd put together to several other ministers, who were interested in sharing the process with grieving members of their congregations.

"Will you make it into a book that we can buy?" she asked. How could I say no? I titled it *Praying You Goodbye*.

At the urging of another friend who worked in Hospice Care, I created another version. "*Praying You Goodbye* is lovely for Christians," she said, "but I'd love to have one for people of other faiths, as well as people with no particular faith." *How Do I Say Goodbye?* was born of her request.

Seven years later, I lost my dad, and headed back to Well of Mercy with a blank *Praying You Goodbye*. That tear-splotched copy was my faithful companion in my grief and still holds the spirit of my father's presence.

In the past 15 years, I've had a number of people tell me this book has made a real difference in their ongoing healing from the loss of a loved one, or, sometimes, a pending loss—and not only through death, but also divorce and other separations.

I'm sharing it with you in the hopes that it will offer you similar comfort and grace, no matter what kind of loss you have experienced, how long ago it happened, or where you are in the process. You may even find that coming back to this book again after some years have passed will offer new insights and deepened healing, wholeness, and gratitude.

How to Get the Most From This Book

SOME GUIDANCE ON LOCATION

Well of Mercy, where I grieved, healed, and celebrated my mother's life, has a Prayer Path with seating at intervals along its wooded trail and a stream with a peaceful, healing murmur. This, or another retreat location, can feel very nurturing. However, this ritual can be done anywhere that provides space, comfort, and privacy, including your own home. If possible, do give yourself time before, during, and/or after each section to spend at least a little time in the natural world, which has healing properties of its own to offer.

SOME GUIDANCE ON TIMING

While I used this ritual soon after my mother, and later, my father, died, it's helpful at any time after you have lost a loved one, even years later. It can also be used to prepare for such a loss, giving you insight into possible conversations you might want to have.

Grief has its own timetable, and so do you. You may choose to move through the entire process in one day, or over a weekend. Or you may want to space it out over months. You may want unlimited time with all the sections, or to set a timer for ten- or fifteen-minute containers of time for each. Listen to yourself and trust yourself.

And follow what James W. Pennebaker, Ph.D., a renowned researcher in writing as a healing process, calls "the flip out rule": "If you feel that your writing about a particular topic is too much for you to handle, then do not write about it. If you know that you aren't ready to address a particularly painful topic, write about something else. When you are ready, then tackle it. If you feel that you will flip out by writing, don't write." (from *Writing to Heal: A Guided Journal for Recovering from Trauma. and Emotional Upheaval.* Oakland, CA: New Harbinger Press, 2004)

SOME GUIDANCE ON WHAT TO HAVE WITH YOU

You'll need a pen or pencil and this book. Have some tissues handy, too. You may also want a photograph of your loved one, and/or a small talisman, perhaps an item that belonged to him or her. In addition, gather items of comfort and nurturing. Cozy socks, comfortable clothing (perhaps even an article that belonged to your loved one), a warm, soothing beverage, comforting music, scented lotion and/or bubble bath—anything you can think of that will allow you to treat yourself tenderly.

You may also want to have a close friend or family member nearby or on call. While solitude allows a sense of safety and freedom to engage fully, words of comfort and a well-timed hug can make an enormous difference.

SOME GUIDANCE ON THE PROCESS

No matter what location you choose, you may want to complete each section in a different spot. This will give the process a journey-like quality—and it is a journey.

Take as long as you need. As you travel through each emotion, don't worry about whether you "have already said that." Some of these themes are related; there will be some overlap. That doesn't matter. Each prompt will give you the opportunity to say what you need to say.

Some of your regrets, resentments, etc. may be directed at another person rather than your loved one. Some of them may bring up feelings of shame. I discovered, to my surprise, that I resented that my husband's parents were both still living while my mother was not. My first instinct was to be ashamed of such a "bad, mean" feeling. Then I stopped myself. Would I be so hard on another human being who was grieving? Who are we to judge ourselves harshly for our feelings, especially in the face of the loss of a loved one? I believe the Creator's deep love for us is a love for each atom of our being, even the parts that may feel unacceptable to us.

As you move through this process, be compassionate. Allow yourself to experience whatever feelings show up—just listen and let them be there. Hear the still small voice whispering that you are loved just as you are in each moment. There are no good or bad, right or wrong, appropriate or inappropriate feelings. Your feelings are not you; they're simply neural responses moving through you. You may feel sad, silly, relieved, grateful, angry… Good! You're still alive!

After you've finished each section, read over what you wrote, perhaps even aloud, using your loved one's name: "Mother, I regret that I'll never eat another of your home-canned pears from the tree in our back yard." "I regret that I never told you it was your reading me *Hailstones and Halibut Bones* and 'Custard the Dragon' when I was little that let me know I could be a poet."

Pause for a few moments, listening for any words your Creator, your inner wisdom—or your loved one—may have for you. You may want to write down these words and/or look at your loved one's photograph or talisman as you reflect. You may even experience a sense that your loved one is healing as you heal. (More on this in Appendix I.)

Before going to the next prompt, engage in some physical movement. This is an integral part of your ceremony, giving your mind, body, and spirit time to rest and integrate. If you're outdoors, walk to another bench or resting spot. If you're indoors, yoga, dancing, stretching, or any other form of movement works. Allow yourself to breathe deeply as you move. Notice your surroundings and the sensations in your body. Then continue on.

Lastly, remember that this is your honoring of your relationship with your loved one(s). Adapt this ritual in any way that works for you—make it your own. One of my writing students, Lori LeRoy, wrote to tell me that she used the "Blessing" section to think back through the years and come up with 50 blessings for her parents to celebrate their 50th wedding anniversary. She added a few photos and had a beautiful keepsake to give them.

Beginning

As you begin, pause and take a few deep breaths. Close your eyes and check in with your body, starting with your feet, connected to the earth, and traveling slowly through each inch of you up to the top of your head, connected with the infinite sky. You are home, right here where you are. Give thanks for your body, mind, and spirit, and then open your eyes and focus your attention on your surroundings, using all your senses. You may want to say a prayer or recite a passage, Scriptural or otherwise, that has meaning for you. Here's one I love:

> *Shout for joy, you heavens;*
> *rejoice, you earth;*
> *burst into song, you mountains!*
> *For the Lord comforts his people*
> *and will have compassion on his afflicted ones.*
> *But Zion said, "The Lord has forsaken me,*
> *the Lord has forgotten me."*
> *"Can a mother forget the baby at her breast*
> *and have no compassion on the child she has borne?*
> *Though she may forget,*
> *I will not forget you!*
> *See, I have engraved you on the palms of my hands;*
> *your walls are ever before me."*

Isaiah 49:13-16

When you're ready, turn the page.

Regret

These things I remember as I pour out my soul:
how I used to go to the house of God
under the protection of the Mighty One
with shouts of joy and praise among the festive throng.

Psalm 42:4

Immediately the rooster crowed the second time.
Then Peter remembered the word Jesus had spoken to him:
"Before the rooster crows twice, you will disown me
three times." And he broke down and wept.

Mark 14:72

What have you lost? What words and actions would you undo if you could? What was left undone, unsaid, unfinished between you and your loved one, or for your loved one?

I regretted that my mother wouldn't be at my children's graduations or weddings, that I wouldn't ever taste another one of her cherry pies, that I spent so many years holding grudges against her for things she'd done when I was a child, that she hadn't ever seen Monet's garden at Giverny as she had longed to do, that she hadn't been happier, that she would miss the crabapple trees blooming, that I couldn't ever call her again when a poem got published or I won an award or I needed one of her recipes...

You may find that adding the words "that I didn't ever tell you" and/or "that you will miss" is useful as you voice your regrets to and about your loved one.

15

Complete this phrase: I regret (that) . . .

Resentment

Then Abimelech called Abraham in and said, "What have you done to us? How have I wronged you that you have brought such great guilt upon me and my kingdom? You have done things to me that should never be done."

Genesis 20:9

The older brother became angry and refused to go in. So his father went out and pleaded with him. But he answered his father, "Look! All these years I've been slaving for you and never disobeyed your orders. Yet you never gave me even a young goat so I could celebrate with my friends. But when this son of yours who has squandered your property with prostitutes comes home, you kill the fattened calf for him!"

Luke 15:28-30

The path to freedom from resentful thoughts is often *through* them, rather than around them. Some of us have large resentments; most of us have small ones. Don't worry if you discover petty resentments from long ago. We all have a child inside clutching to things that are downright, well, childish. I found myself listing grievances like: "Mother, I resent that you wouldn't let me see *Butterflies Are Free* when I was 15. No one else's mother cared that the movie showed Goldie Hawn in her underwear."

You may even find yourself chuckling, as I did, at the indignant child inside who's still upset that her bedtime was earlier than her brothers'. Once you have acknowledged your resentments, you have a new freedom to let them go.

Complete this phrase: I resent (that) . . .

Anger

Anger is such an uncomfortable emotion, isn't it? Yet it is one of the stages of grief Elisabeth Kübler-Ross wrote about in her book *On Death and Dying*. Each stage is necessary to claim and experience if we are to make our way to acceptance. You may feel anger at God for taking your loved one away. You may feel anger toward others for things they said or didn't say, did or didn't do. You may feel angry with yourself, or even with your loved one.

I discovered I was still angry that my mother had told me a number of times in my childhood that she hadn't wanted me. As an adult, I understood that most women with three children under five—each born in a different city, no less—wouldn't be happy to be pregnant again. But it still stung. I was also angry that my mother lost interest in living as she aged. Why didn't she fight for more time with her children and grandchildren?

How good it feels to name the anger, then lay it down.

Complete this phrase: I'm angry (that or about) . . .

Sadness

There is a time for everything, and a season for every activity
under the heavens: a time to be born and a time to die,
a time to plant and a time to uproot...
a time to weep and a time to laugh,
a time to mourn and a time to dance...

Ecclesiastes 3:1, 2 and 4

For I wrote you out of great distress and anguish of heart
and with many tears, not to grieve you
but to let you know the depth of my love for you.

2 Corinthians 2:4

How healing it was for me to sit by a beautiful flowing stream and let myself be sad, to give up being strong and brave for a while.

I was now motherless; the word itself made me sad. I would never again hear my mother's voice gladden when she realized it was me calling on the phone. I'd never again see her dry her hands on her apron. I'd never again see her waving as I pulled out of her driveway. For me, regret was more about the big losses, and sadness about the little ones. How is it for you?

Remember that repetition is a natural, even necessary, part of the process. Be gentle as you let go and let your sadness be; own it as an expression of your love.

Complete this phrase: I'm sad (that or about) . . .

Fear

When I am afraid, I put my trust in you.

Psalm 56:3

When the disciples saw him walking on the lake, they
were terrified. "It's a ghost," they said, and cried out in fear.
But Jesus immediately said to them:
"Take courage! It is I. Don't be afraid."
"Lord, if it's you," Peter replied,
"tell me to come to you on the water."
"Come," he said.
Then Peter got down out of the boat, walked on the water
and came toward Jesus. But when he saw the wind, he was
afraid and, beginning to sink, cried out, "Lord, save me!"

Matthew 14:26-30

Most of us are much more comfortable being regretful, resentful, angry, or sad than afraid. Fear makes us feel small and vulnerable.

"Mother," I wrote, "I'm afraid that I will forget the sound of your voice." "I'm afraid now that you're not here as a shield between me and my own death."

Think of these words of Eleanor Roosevelt's as you write this list: "You gain strength, courage, and confidence by every experience in which you really stop to look fear in the face. You are able to say to yourself, 'I have lived through this horror. I can take the next thing that comes along.'"

You are not alone, and you are stronger and larger than any fear.

Complete this phrase: I'm afraid (that or of) . . .

Forgiveness

"For I will forgive their wickedness
and will remember their sins no more."

Jeremiah 31:34b

Then Peter came up to Jesus and asked,
"Lord, how many times shall I forgive
my brother or sister who sins against me?
Up to seven times?"
Jesus answered, "I tell you, not seven times,
but seventy-seven times."

Matthew 18:21-22

No matter how much you loved the person you have lost, no matter how close you were, it's inevitable that you were at times hurt and angry at things this person said or did. Here is your chance to let go of any hurt, anger, and resentment you may have experienced. If nothing comes to mind, you might want to look back at what you wrote in the "Resentment" and "Anger" sections.

I used to think forgiveness was a gift to the person I was forgiving; it took me years to see that it was an even greater gift to myself. Just writing the words "I forgive you, Mother" made me feel lighter.

Notice the lightness you experience in your body, mind, and spirit as you write out your forgiveness.

Complete this phrase: I forgive you (for) . . .

Reconciliation

Then he [Joseph] threw his arms around his brother Benjamin
and wept, and Benjamin embraced him, weeping.

Genesis 45:14

Therefore, if you are offering your gift at the altar
and there remember that your brother or sister has something
against you, leave your gift there in front of the altar.
First go and be reconciled to them;
then come and offer your gift.

Matthew 5:23-24

Just as our loved ones have wronged us sometimes, we have at times hurt, angered, and disappointed our loved ones.

If there is anything that you regret having said or done, you can now ask your loved one's forgiveness and experience reconciliation. It's time to let go of any guilt and shame you may be harboring.

"Mother, please forgive me for not realizing how happy a letter or phone call would have made you," I wrote. "I ask your forgiveness for not appreciating how hard you worked to raise four children born within five years of each other."

Imagine your loved one's arms around you, embracing you with forgiveness, just as, in the passage above, Joseph embraced his brother Benjamin. Let yourself experience the peace that flows from this moment of reconciliation.

Complete this phrase: Please forgive me for . . .
OR I ask your forgiveness for . . .

Gratitude

Many, LORD my God, are the wonders you have done,
the things you planned for us. None can compare with you;
were I to speak and tell of your deeds,
they would be too many to declare.

Psalm 40:5

Rejoice always; pray continually; give thanks in all
circumstances, for this is God's will for you in Christ Jesus.

1 Thessalonians 5:16-18

After walking through the many emotions that accompany loss, what often appears is gratitude. For at the depth of our grief is the love we will always feel for those who have gone before us, leaving us beautiful memories and bountiful gifts.

I didn't know where to begin capturing even a fraction of my gratitude for my mother's presence in my life. But as I sat next to a peaceful stream, I remembered an October afternoon about six months before she died from the Lewy Body disease which robbed her of her physical abilities and her lucidity—except for occasional glimmers. After feeding her lunch, I'd held her hands. In that moment of simply being with her, deep gratitude welled up in me. It was such a precious time, witnessing her let go of so much with such grace and courage. I couldn't have imagined that just sitting in a patch of sunshine, holding my mother's hands and smiling into her eyes, could make me feel so happy. And gift of all gifts, in that moment, my mother spoke. "I'm so grateful."

What are you grateful for?

Complete this phrase: I'm grateful (for or that) . . .

Rejoicing

Weeping may endure for a night, but joy cometh in the morning.

Psalm 30:5b (from the King James Bible)

Very truly I tell you, you will weep and mourn
while the world rejoices.
You will grieve, but your grief will turn to joy.
A woman giving birth to a child has pain because her time
has come; but when her baby is born she forgets the anguish
because of her joy that a child is born into the world.
So with you: Now is your time of grief,
but I will see you again and you will rejoice,
and no one will take away your joy.

John 16:20-22

"Weeping may endure for a night, but joy cometh in the morning." This particular wording from Psalm 30 has long been one of my favorite Scriptural passages. Even as I grieved, I rejoiced that my mother had come to stay with us for a week when my daughter was born; that all five of us, her children, were with her on the day she died; that I can continue her traditions, like homemade Orange Rolls for Easter breakfast; and that she not only got to celebrate her 50th wedding anniversary with her entire family present, but also, the priest at Mass was one who had known her for nearly forty of those fifty years.

Grief and joy are often intermingled. Write about what brings you joy, even now, in this time of loss.

Complete this phrase: I rejoice (that) . . .

Blessing

About Joseph he [Moses] said: "May the Lord bless his land
with the precious dew from heaven above and with the deep
waters that lie below; with the best the sun brings forth
and the finest the moon can yield; with the choicest gifts
of the ancient mountains and the fruitfulness
of the everlasting hills; with the best gifts of the earth
and its fullness and the favor of him
who dwelt in the burning bush."

Deuteronomy 33:13-16a

From the fullness of His grace, we all have received
one blessing after another.

John 1:16

No matter who we are, our lives are filled with blessings. And our loved one blessed us in numerous ways in his or her lifetime. It was a great joy, as part of my ritual, to speak directly to my mother, blessing her for blessing me. I chose to write a "Bless you" for each year of my mother's life. Here are a few:

 * Bless you for being a model of strength and passion.
 * Bless you for noticing how much I loved *Mary Poppins* when I was a little, and, on no particular occasion, leaving a new Mary Poppins blanket on my bed for me to discover.
 * Bless you for making my favorite foods when I visited.
 * Bless you for thinking I should send my daughter's baby pictures to Gerber because they would surely want to use them in their ads.

How has your loved one blessed you?

Complete this phrase: Bless you (for) . . .

Releasing

Shake off your dust; rise up, sit enthroned, O Jerusalem.
Free yourself from the chains on your neck,
Daughter Zion, now a captive.

Isaiah 52:2

He said to her, "Daughter, your faith has healed you.
Go in peace and be freed from your suffering."

Mark 5:34

What have you been holding onto that you are now ready to release? It may be a belief you have about how you are supposed to feel about the death of your loved one.

I remember a moment, a few months after my mother's funeral, when I caught myself dancing with abandon on the beach at sunset. I realized, with a start, that my mother was dead, and stopped abruptly, feeling terribly guilty for being so happy. It was a relief to let go of my guilt and my sense that I was not supposed to be experiencing joy. I could be sad when I was sad, and happy when I was happy.

You may also wish to release some, or even all, of the things that you are angry, resentful, and/or regretful about.

Sometimes a metaphorical representation of this release can be very freeing. You could drop a leaf in a stream or skip a stone across water, or choose some other physical motion. I decided to fling a leaf for each "release"—I dropped them onto the ground so I wouldn't clog the stream with all I had been holding onto!

Complete this phrase: I now let go of . . .

Treasuring

One of the musicals my mother loved, *Crazy for You*, contains the song "They Can't Take That Away from Me." All that we love remains a part of us forever. What about your loved one will you treasure always? What will you keep, as the Bible says, "for the generations to come"? What will you pass on?

I now wear a ring that was my mother's. Objects can be treasured reminders of the ones we love. I will also treasure my mother's passion for show tunes, and the fact that she was the only one on this earth to ever call me "Mosie," her affectionate derivative of my college nickname, "Mo."

After you write down what you will treasure, if you are outdoors, you may want to find a natural object—a rock, a leaf, a beautiful piece of bark—to take with you as a reminder of this ritual honoring your loved one.

Complete this phrase: I will treasure . . .

Parting

Yet I am always with you; you hold me by my right hand.

Psalm 73:23

Jesus went on to say, "In a little while you will see me no more, and then after a little while you will see me."

John 16:16

Here, at the end of this ritual, pause to take some deep breaths. Be still and just notice the thoughts moving through your mind.

Breathe in and out, and let your emotions ebb and flow, as they'll continue to do. You don't have to try to change them. As the Persian poet Rumi said, "This being human is a guesthouse." Our feelings come, and they go. But our love does not. You have been saying goodbye to your loved one, but you have not been dismissing him or her. He or she is woven into your life forever.

> *We are speaking of love. A leaf, a handful of seed—*
> *begin with these, learn a little what it is to love.*
> *First, a leaf, a fall of rain, then someone to receive*
> *what a leaf has taught you, what a fall of rain*
> *has ripened. No easy process, understand;*
> *it could take a lifetime, it has mine,*
> *and still I've never mastered it–*
> *I only know how true it is: that love*
> *is a chain of love, as nature is a chain of life.*
>
> Truman Capote

We are speaking of love, aren't we? You and your loved one will forever remain a part of that "chain of life" and "chain of love."

At this time, do you have any additional words for or about your loved one? Is there anything else you'd like to say? If so, use the following pages to do that.

You may choose to finish with the same prayer or passage with which you began, or another that is meaningful to you, perhaps The Lord's Prayer or these heartening words:

> For I know the plans I have for you," declares the Lord,
> "plans to prosper you and not to harm you,
> plans to give you hope and a future."
>
> Jeremiah 29:11

Afterwards, it may be helpful to stretch or walk a bit as you move back into your life.

Godspeed. You do not walk alone.

APPENDIX I
The Healing Benefits of Writing

One of the first people to believe that writing had the potential to heal was New York Jungian psychologist Ira Progoff. Back in the 1960s, he noticed that his clients who kept journals recovered more quickly than those who did not.

By the middle of the 1980s, Dr. James Pennebaker, a research psychologist at the University of Texas at Austin, had discovered through numerous studies that writing about difficult emotions and traumatic experiences "resulted in improved moods, more positive outlook, and greater physical health" (as noted in his book *Opening Up: The Healing Power of Expressing Emotion*). Subsequent studies showed expressive writing can lead to stronger immune function, lowered blood pressure, and fewer doctor visits, as well as reducing symptoms of asthma and rheumatoid arthritis. In 2004, Pennebaker came out with a book called *Writing to Heal: A Guided Journal for Recovering from Trauma and Emotional Upheaval* that I use as a resource for myself and my writing classes. (You can read about Dr. James W. Pennebaker and my experience with his work in an article by Vivé Griffith at www.utexas.edu/features/archive/2005/writing.html. And you can order Pennebaker's helpful book for $20 at journaltherapy.com/product/writing-to-heal/.)

In my own journey, and as I've worked with clients and students over the past 20-plus years, I've become passionate about the power of writing as a healing process. Here are specific benefits writing about grief and trauma can provide, whether you're journaling, journeying through this book, or shaping memories and reflections into stories, essays, and/or poems:

◊ A quieting of the mind, which can lead to less stress and better sleep
◊ Space for reflection
◊ A gain in insight and perspective
◊ The fulfillment of participating in a creative act

◊ The ability to connect with others through our stories (As Sadie F. Dingfelder says in "Our stories, ourselves," an article posted in the American Psychological Association's *Monitor on Psychology*, "Every story is a gift, a little part of yourself that you share with the audience" and "Who doesn't like gifts?")

◊ Distance, allowing you to put troubling thoughts and emotions outside you

◊ Containment of difficult emotions (As Denver psychotherapist Kathleen Adams, founder/director of the Center for Journal Therapy and author of *Journal to the Self* says, "Know that when you write, you are moving thoughts, feelings and energy out of your mind and body and into a neutral, receptive place where they will be stored safely for you.")

◊ Access to the full range of your emotions (As Seattle poet and family practice physician Peter Pereira, author of the poetry collections *Saying the World* and *What's Written on the Body*, puts it, writing gives us "the dual function of allowing us to contain as well as access intense feelings, emotions, and life events.")

◊ Healing not just for yourself, but your family as well (In an article titled "Healing the Wounds of Your Ancestors" in *The Huffington Post*, Dr. Judith Rich explores the beautiful idea that, as we heal, we heal not only the generations that come after us, but also our ancestors.)

◊ A reclaiming of power, being active rather than passive (Denise Cullen discusses this process in an article called "The Power of the Pen" in *The Age Online*.)

◊ Catharsis

◊ An opportunity to remake an experience and find meaning in it (Lulu Miller writes about this in "Editing Your Life Stories Can Create Happier Endings" in *Shots: Health News from NPR*.)

APPENDIX II
Sample Writings

When I'm dealing with a tough time, I turn to words to move through the full range of emotions and get to the proverbial other side. Following are some poems and prose pieces that served as containers for my regret, resentment, anger, sadness, and fear as I reached forward into forgiveness, reconciliation, gratitude, rejoicing, blessing, releasing, and the treasuring of all I loved about my mother. I find shaping even the most challenging of experiences into "created things" to be very cathartic, and it connects me to others experiencing loss as well.

Use these writings, if you like, as inspiration to create your own as you continue your journey of grieving, healing, and gratitude.

When the Leaves Are in the Water

When my brother and I walked
through these woods, he pointed out
subtleties of bark and branches,
read growth rings, spoke of drought
and rainy years. Said I look

like Mother. What I love
about trees: they endure
the seasons. I yearn
to be Sweet Gum, Sugar Maple.
My brother named me

Ironwood, divined my rusting
heart, too hard to yield
forgiveness. Would we agree on Oak,
my gallnuts early griefs
painstakingly transformed?

Arriving at the creek bank,
I let silt run through
my fingers, minute bits of pebble
with unseen roughness.
I wasn't looking when my hands

turned into hers. I plunge them
into cold creek water.
I once thought
forgiving her was clean,
balsam on a wound

to make it heal. It's more
like washing hands
before a meal. I have to do it
over and over: forgiveness
to the third power. I feel

it's time, but loss spirals
deeper each succeeding
season. What will I be without
my holy anger—stripped bare
like the skeleton of a tree,

my stipule scars, my leaf
scars showing? Trees are born
to nakedness—I'm not ready.
My brother told me
the Cherokee believe

it's a time of great power
when the leaves are in the water.
I fling in handfuls of hard
memories, watch the current
carry them away.

The Color of Crushed Strawberries

"My mother is dressed in a dress
the color of crushed strawberries."
~ Edward Hirsch

My mother is dressed in a flannel nightgown
the color of faded morning glories, on her knees
on the hardwood floor of her bedroom
mumbling Hail Mary's, begging forgiveness
for the sin of not wanting
five children's worth of work.

My mother is dressed in an apron
the color of ashes, by the stove
frying sugared parsnips, spearing chunks
of city chicken, serving salted complaints
about our not appreciating her.

My mother is dressed in corduroy pants
the color of sodden newspapers, on a stepladder,
the smell of ammonia strong, the window
panes squeaking, the streaks meekly disappearing
in the face of her furious rubbing.

My mother is dressed in a raveled sweater
the color of old snow, scrubbing socks
on a washboard. She is not dressed
in her wedding rings. They hang
on the Virgin Mary's white ceramic hands,
the palms together, pointing upward in supplication.

How I longed to see her in
lipstick the color of crushed strawberries,
humming as she dressed in blue watered silk.

But summer upon summer,
after we'd bruised our knees
on the packed soil of the fields,
bent over the sink hulling
entire afternoons away,
she let me
wield the potato masher
in the copper-bottomed pot
filled with the makings
of next winter's jam.

All week, I have been wanting to write about...

I wrote this journal entry in February of 2002, about three months be-
fore my mother died. I'd just come back from a visit with her, and had
been reading Thomas Lynch's The Undertaking: Life Studies from
the Dismal Trade. *Lynch is a poet as well as an undertaker, and the*
book is a lyrical examination of the way we as a culture face (or refuse
to face) death. The book and the visit were roiling about in me, and it
was a great comfort to me to spill out my thoughts and feelings:

All week I have been wanting to write about my mother in a col-
or of lipstick she would never have worn, rouge on her cheeks,
her hair styled in a trendy wisp of bangs—all for me, thanks to
some well-intentioned staff member who knew "Pat" had a visit-
ing daughter and "fixed her up," my mother in a wheelchair with
no use of her hands and it broke my heart, that lipstick, seeing my
mother looking so unlike herself. She rarely wore makeup and
never, never that color—she was a true red.

I wish I'd saved her lipsticks—the really nice ones in gold cases—
I must call Dad today and ask. If it's not too late. I don't know
what I'll do with them. I don't know what to do with this desire
to take care of my mother. How could I handle the bathrooming,
the feeding, the physical therapy? And my dad is happy in Erie,
especially now that the Sisters of Saint Benedict have adopted him

to do maintenance and repairs at the House of Healing. He's so happy to have problems to tinker with—the passion in his voice as he spoke of finally sawing through a rusted old pipe! I never heard him talk of my mother in that way—she was a problem he couldn't solve.

And what about my mother? I want to be there for her and I'm so far away. Reading about social and metabolic death in The *Undertaking*, I see my mother isn't dead to me, as she is to many others. That's why I want to be with her when she dies. I want to hold her hand during that passage and I'm so scared it won't go that way. This is what I really want, not that gold lipstick case.

No, I want that, too, I want it all and some days I am not a big enough container for all I want. Enough. All week I have been wanting to write about the snow falling and what an inconvenience it felt like, worrying about my flight being delayed and a little voice inside crying *You don't even see how beautiful it is! Can you stop and look?* But I didn't.

Can I write to the other side of sadness? If I just take it all as life, this moment, I don't have to. Sad is sad. "This room and everything in it"—words from that beautiful poem by Li-Young Lee, came floating into my morning pages today and that Steve Martin/ Lily Tomlin movie—*All of me, why not take all of me*—what if I didn't care that my mother was wearing the wrong lipstick? What if it was exactly right—or better, if things weren't wrong or right, if they just were.

Writing this journal entry also spurred me into action. I called and told my father how much it mattered to me to be present at my mother's death. His father had died while my dad was at the Coast Guard Academy, and his mother had written him with news some weeks after the fact, so I was afraid he wouldn't think to call me.

I was able to be with my mother at the end of her life, and articulating these thoughts helped me to accept her death just as it was when the time came.

The Last of Your Pond's Skin Cream

One day soon—
Next Sunday? A week
from Wednesday?—I will smooth
the last of your Pond's Skin Cream
over the cheekbones I got from you.

Two days after you died, Dad gave me
the four jars, maybe five, stacked
in the bathroom cabinet, each bought—
I've no doubt—on sale, dated month/year
by your ever-ready stub of a grease pencil.

I could have stroked some on your skin;
I bet the nursing staff never did that.
Water under the dam, you'd say. Since,
I have been so dutiful, each jar
in its due time. You'd be so proud.

It has seemed as though this stash, this scent
of you would never end; I have been
by turn sparing and slapdash, worrying
only a bit about expiration dates, the cream's
slight yellow cast. When was the last

time my fingers touched your face?
No matter, as they dip into each day's
portion. It's going on three years now,
and a lone jar of your home-canned pears
still sits on our pantry shelf. How we

loved them, the summers they held!
But surely I can bring myself
to see this through—the last jar
of Pond's is deep but I see
more of the bottom each morning.

When We Parted, All That Was Really Left...

all that was really left
   the tremor of your hands

all that was really
      real: the oxygen tank, the nurse
      who brushed your hair, that broken-handled
      pink plastic hairbrush,
      nylon bristles half-gone—why did you never
      buy yourself a new hairbrush, why did I
      never notice, right there
      on your vanity, each year of
      my childhood, dwindling

all that was
      to say how grateful I am
      for that last night, sleeping there
      on two pushed-together chairs
      next to your bed, hearing
      your labored breath,
      that you held on
      until all five
      of your children arrived

all that
      and how I told you
      Perry Como
      would sing for you
      in heaven—my last words

      Now that you're gone
all
      that is really left
      is everything
      I remember

Eyes-in-the-Back-of-Her-Head Stew

In one of my most treasured memories, my mother stands with her back to me, cooking supper. I am three years old, and have propelled myself into the kitchen on my wooden riding horse. Climbing off, I stare at the painted circus animals chasing each other around the colorful metal wheels. "What's this?" I ask, pointing, knowing very well what it is.

My mother turns to look. "Zebra."

I let her turn away before asking again, "What's this?"

"Elephant." Then lion, then bear.

I keep going around and around the wheel, sometimes skipping animals just to see if she's really paying attention. She keeps turning and answering, until a moment I ask yet again, "What's this?" and she answers correctly without looking around.

I am utterly amazed. "How did you do that?"

"I have eyes in the back of my head."

"You do not!" I say. "Show me."

She laughs. I keep on, pressing for an answer. "But how did you know? You knew without looking!"

"It's because I'm a mother," she says. "Someday you'll be a mother, and you'll be able to do it too."

Perhaps I remember this incident so vividly because it was the first time I encountered the idea that I would actually grow up, that I could someday be a mother too. It seemed impossible, and yet, there was my mother, so sure of it she could say so in the midst of making stew.

For Mother, As I Sort Through This Old Box of Clothes Saved for a Granddaughter

I remember sitting in the tub,
you washing my hair, a halo
around your head where light

met the steam. I was telling you
how much I loved being eight,
that I wanted to be eight forever.

And then I was nine and so happy
to be nine I wanted that age
to last forever too, then ten,

the years clicking by like Hail Mary's
on your rosary beads till I would want
nothing more than to leave you.
But that year, my eighth, you bought me
this candy-striped pink and white dress
with a whale on it.

I remember wanting to cry
when I tried it on the next summer
and it no longer fit.

Though I didn't tell you,
you came home one day carrying
the identical dress, striped in blue,

in the next larger size. Proving
something about love I've never
found words to thank you for.

Gift

"You will receive a gift," the workshop leader tells us. We do not know what it will be, nor when it will arrive, but at some point during this afternoon, as we explore "How to Have an Inner Life that Supports Your Outer Life," the gift will come. Our chairs form a circle around a candle, a small fire to connect us to all human beings who have gathered for all time around a center of light and warmth to share their stories. We share our own to form this community of souls on this particular day—why we have come, what is in our hearts.

"This morning," I say, when it is my turn, "I got an email from my father telling me that they were calling in Hospice for my mother." Hospice. A clean-to-the-bone word, shocking despite the fact that we have known, my four siblings and I, that our mother's disease is terminal.

Of course, I'd thought as I read his words, I couldn't attend this writing workshop, even if I had been looking forward to it for months, even if it was being led by one of my writing heroes, Christina Baldwin, a forerunner in the journal writing field whose *Life's Companion* is one of the most dog-eared, well-worn books on my shelves. Not only was I numb with grief, but I also had to prepare for a 600-mile trip to my hometown for an indefinite amount of time. There were items to pack, care arrangements to be made for my children, appointments to cancel.

But I believe in the power of the word, don't I? I've always said writing was a medicine for times such as this, and so I have come anyway. And after we've wound our way around the circle, cast our stories into the flame, Christina gives us a very simple, meditative exercise with which to begin: Close your eyes. Take a deep breath—a reminder to be in your body. Open your eyes. Catch an image. Let go. Write five minutes. This will be, she says, "most delicious if you have no idea what to say."

My eyes rest on a tree outside the window. Yes. My pen meets paper here. I've always liked being outside more than in, from when I was a small girl who loved the small woods behind her backyard more than her house.

And this thought turns into words about the times I have fallen asleep in the dark in a place I've never been before. There were a number of these on the whirlwind, three-week trip from Erie, Pennsylvania, to San Francisco and back when I was 22.

I remember being lulled to sleep by the Green River, which I could hear but not see. Later, there was a bed and breakfast in Bath, North Carolina, which I didn't know overlooked the Pamlico River until daylight, when I peeked out my bedroom window. I practically ran downstairs with my journal, grabbing a cup of coffee on my way out to the bench that beckoned below a willow right beside the river. Sunlight rippled. What delight.

But, oh, the best of these morning surprises was most definitely the one on the 52-hour Greyhound bus trip I took a few years before my cross country adventure. I was 20, on my way to spend the summer in Flagstaff, Arizona, with my oldest brother, who was going to graduate school there. I'd never been to the Southwest. I fell asleep somewhere in Kansas with my face against the bus window, awoke to the sun rising over red rock country—a sight so foreign and so beautiful that I gasped out loud right there in my seat, awestruck by this new landscape. And as I wrote about this moment, out came the words, "This is what it will be like for my mother." There it was, my gift from the retreat.

I carried this gift with me up three long, rainy highways, through the mountains and two tunnels, into the room where my mother lay asleep, her breathing supported by oxygen. It lay with me on the two chairs pushed together into a makeshift bed that I took over from my sister. It carried me through the next days with an easy grace, this certainty that my mother would soon be filled with that joy.

Leaves, Wind, Light, Wings

This fall morning, through my open back door,
I watch a flurry of leaves swirl through sun,
golden themselves, scraps of pure light against
exultant blue. Past the windows rush more,
their shadows dark behind closed blinds, driven
as birds, yes, geese winging their sure way south.
The world is so beautiful, even as it reels
through our grasp. Here in this room, wearing

a green dress that was my mother's, I will
open all my windows and doors as if
I have nothing to hide, imagining her
happy at last, her hands raised high. She is
shaking the trees to make this loveliness.
She is the wind, the leaves. She is the geese.

Made in the USA
Lexington, KY
31 August 2018